SAFETY PLAYS

David Bird • Marc Smith

MASTER POINT PRESS • TORONTO

Master Point Press
22 Lower Village Gate
Toronto, Ontario, Canada
M5P 3L7
(416) 932-9766   Internet www.pathcom.com/~raylee/

Distributed in the USA by Barricade Books
150 Fifth Avenue, Suite 700
New York, NY 10011
(800) 59-BOOKS

Canadian Cataloguing in Publication Data
Bird, David, 1946-
Safety plays

(Bridge technique; 3)
ISBN 1-894154-19-3

1. Contract bridge - Dummy plays. I. Smith, Marc, 1960- . II Title.
III. Series: Bird, David, 1946-. Bridge technique; 3

GV1282.435 B73 2000   795. 41'.53   C99-932383-0

Cover design and Interior: Olena S. Sullivan
Editor: Ray Lee

Printed and bound in Canada

1 2 3 4 5 6 7   07 06 05 04 03 02 01 00

CONTENTS

Bridge Technique Series

Entry Management

Tricks with Trumps

Safety Plays

Available September, 2000

Eliminations and Throw Ins

Deceptive Card Play

Planning in Suit Contracts

Available March, 2001

Planning in Notrump Contracts

Planning in Defense

Squeezes for Everyone

Available September, 2001

Defensive Signaling

Reading the Cards

Tricks with Finesses

CHAPTER 1

What is a Safety Play?

You may think it is stating the obvious to say that declarer's aim is to make enough tricks to fulfill his contract. Yes, but it's surprising how often players put this objective at risk, quite unnecessarily.

A 'safety play' is precisely what the name implies. In some cases, it simply reduces the chances of going down. In other cases, it provides what is known as a 'sure tricks line of play' — that is to say, it guarantees your contract. If you want to draw a comparison, think of a safety play in terms of buying insurance. You don't have to spend the money, and most of the time, nothing bad happens anyway. But for a small premium, you can guard against a catastrophe.

When you perform a safety play within a single suit, you aim to handle your honors in such a way that you can overcome the worst possible distribution of the opponents' cards. This may involve the sacrifice of a trick that would have come your way, had the opponents' cards been favorably placed. No matter. Maximizing your contract's chance of success is the main aim at rubber bridge or IMP scoring.

What would you reaction be if someone asked you the correct way to play this suit?

♡ K 10 6 5 3

♡ A 9 4 2

You should refuse to answer. It depends on how many tricks you require. If you need five tricks from the suit, you will start by cashing one or other honor. Let's say you decide to play the ace. Should this drop the queen or jack from the East hand, the odds favor finessing the ten next (we will see why in Chapter 2).

Suppose instead that you can afford to lose one trick in the suit but the loss of two tricks will cost you the contract. There is a 100% safety play available. Do you know it? You must lead a low card from one hand or other, covering the card that the defender plays or rising with the honor if he shows out. Playing the suit in this way will often cost you an overtrick but it will guarantee the contract.

Let's see a safety play in the context of a full hand:

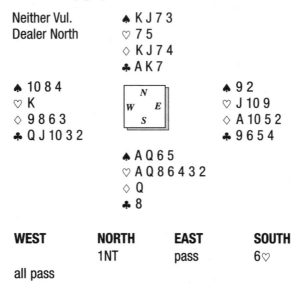

Neither Vul.
Dealer North

North:
♠ K J 7 3
♡ 7 5
◇ K J 7 4
♣ A K 7

West:
♠ 10 8 4
♡ K
◇ 9 8 6 3
♣ Q J 10 3 2

East:
♠ 9 2
♡ J 10 9
◇ A 10 5 2
♣ 9 6 5 4

South:
♠ A Q 6 5
♡ A Q 8 6 4 3 2
◇ Q
♣ 8

WEST	NORTH	EAST	SOUTH
	1NT	pass	6♡
all pass			

You don't like the bidding? Maybe not, but this is a book on cardplay! If West is so inspired as to find a diamond lead, you will have to hope that East holds a doubleton king of trumps. If instead West leads the ♣Q, you can take the opportunity to discard your diamond loser. The contract is then safe unless you lose two trump tricks. You make the safety play of cashing the ace of trumps first, and virtue is rewarded when West's king appears. If the king does not drop, you will re-enter dummy and lead a heart towards the queen. By surrendering a possible overtrick (if East holds king doubleton of trumps) you increase your overall chance of making the slam.

What do you make of this everyday combination?

◇ A 9 6 4

◇ K J 5 2

This holding is regularly misplayed, even by experienced players. How would you tackle the suit? Once again, you should refuse to answer until a question of your own has been answered: 'How many diamond tricks do I need?'

If you need four tricks, your best chance is to find the defenders' cards splitting 3-2 with the queen in the East hand. To take advantage of such a favorable layout (which will occur approximately one third of the time — 34%), you should begin with a low card to the jack. You will score four tricks also when East holds a singleton queen. Many players make the mistake of cashing the ace first. This loses a trick unnecessarily when East holds a singleton queen. Cashing the ace does not help if there is a singleton queen with West because East's 10-8-7-3 is still worth a trick anyway.

Now suppose you need only three tricks from the suit. This combination comes with a 100% guarantee of three tricks, but only if you know the safety play involved! If the suit breaks 3-2, any sensible combinations of plays will produce three tricks. Similarly, if the ten or queen is singleton, cashing either top honor will enable you to develop an easy third trick. The problem is to overcome Q-10-x-x with either defender.

Suppose you don't know the right play. Let's see if we can work it out. How about leading a low card to the jack, the play that nets four tricks when the cards lie favorably? That's no good. When West has a singleton queen, East will score a second trick with his 10-8-7-3. Perhaps this time it is right to start with the ace? No, if West holds Q-10-x-x he will score two tricks.

What else can we try? Let's play the king first. If we continue with a low card to the ace we will lose two tricks when West holds Q-10-x-x. How about continuing with a low card to the nine? Yes, that looks better. We'll test it against Q-10-x-x in either defender's hand:

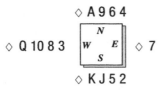

♢ A 9 6 4

♢ Q 10 8 3　♢ 7

♢ K J 5 2

You cash the king, then lead low and cover West's eight with dummy's nine. In this instance, East discards and you have your three diamond tricks. If East had won with the ten or the queen, the suit would have broken 3-2.

Let's give East the diamond length now:

♢ A 9 6 4

♢ 7　♢ Q 10 8 3

♢ K J 5 2

Once again, you cash the king and lead low towards dummy. This time, West shows out, so you rise with the ace and lead a third round towards your remaining ♢J5. East has the queen-ten, but he cannot prevent you from scoring a third diamond trick with your jack.

To finish this introduction, let's put that suit combination into a full hand:

Neither Vul.　　♠ K Q 6
Dealer South　　♡ A 7
　　　　　　　　♢ A 9 6 4
　　　　　　　　♣ K Q 8 5

♠ 9 7 3　　　　　　　　　　　♠ J 10 4 2
♡ J 10 9 4　　　　　　　　　　♡ Q 6 5 2
♢ Q 10 8 3　　　　　　　　　　♢ 7
♣ 7 2　　　　　　　　　　　　♣ 10 9 4 3

　　　　　　　　♠ A 8 5
　　　　　　　　♡ K 8 3
　　　　　　　　♢ K J 5 2
　　　　　　　　♣ A J 6

WEST	NORTH	EAST	SOUTH
			1NT
pass	6NT	all pass	

West leads the ♡J and you pause to plan the play. You have nine top tricks outside the diamond suit. If the contract were an ambitious 7NT you would need four diamond tricks and would lead a low card to the jack, as we saw before. In 6NT you need only three diamond tricks. You should therefore seek a safety play in the diamond suit, to maximize your chance of three tricks (or here, actually guarantee them). As we have seen, you can manage that easily enough. You win the club lead, cash the king of diamonds, and lead a low diamond towards dummy, intending to cover West's card. West has no answer and you are soon scoring up your slam. Had you started diamonds by cashing the ace, the contract would have failed.

You may think that we have spent a little too much time on the description of this one holding: K-J-x-x opposite A-9-x-x. In your bridge-playing career you will encounter vast numbers of suit combinations. Perhaps you have a photographic memory and can instantly recall the sixty pages of small print in the *The Official Encyclopedia of Bridge* that list all the correct safety plays. If not, you will have to work them out at the table. The method is the one that we have described. Test out in your mind the various possibilities and choose the play that will win most often.

Key points

1. Some safety plays guarantee a specific number of tricks from a suit. Others merely maximize your chances of scoring the tricks you need.

2. A safety play may involve losing a trick that does not have to be lost. You concede the trick as an insurance policy against a bad break.

3. The best way to play a particular suit will often depend on how many tricks you need from it.

CHAPTER 2

Playing for Safety in Individual Suits

It would not be productive, in this section of the book, to list countless suit combinations and merely state how they should be played. Instead, our objective is to show you how to work out the right play at the table. We will look only at some of the more interesting holdings, ones that are frequently misplayed. By the end of the chapter we hope you will feel confident to tackle any new combination on your own.

Contracts may be divided into three broad categories: virtually hopeless, normal, apparently invincible. When the contract appears to be a lost cause, you must seek a layout of the opponents' cards that will allow you to prevail. When the contract appears to be cold, ask yourself: 'What can go wrong?' Perhaps your contract is at risk only when the trumps break 5-0. Very well, look for a way to guard against this evil distribution.

On many of the suit combinations that follow, players tend to err solely because they fail to foresee any potential problem.

The opponents hold the jack

Suppose you are playing in six hearts with one obvious side-suit loser and this trump suit:

♡ A 7 5

```
    N
W       E
    S
```

♡ K Q 10 9 4 2

It's amazing how many players start drawing trumps by cashing the ace. Around 95% of the time, they survive this inaccuracy. The suit breaks 2-2 or 3-1, or East has all four trumps and they can take a marked finesse against the jack. However, 5% of the time, West will hold all four trumps. 'I don't believe it!' declarer exclaims, as he goes down.

There is no excuse at all for misplaying such a combination. If you stop to ask yourself 'What can go wrong?' you will come up with the answer that trumps might break 4-0. It costs nothing to play a high heart from your hand first and, having done so, you will be able to play the suit for no losers whatever happens.

The opponents hold the jack and ten

Suppose you need to avoid a loser in this suit:

♡ A 7 5

```
    N
W       E
    S
```

♡ K Q 9 6 4 2

Which honor would you play first? The contract is at risk only if one of the defenders holds J-10-7-4. If West has this holding, there is nothing you can do about it. Your loud complaints of bad luck will be justified. You can, however, pick up the suit when East holds all four trumps. To do this, you must cash the ace first, leaving your K-Q-9 sitting over East's two honors. By leading twice towards the South hand, finessing the nine if East follows low, you can prevent him from scoring a trick in the suit.

The only difference between the last two combinations is the absence or presence of the ten. However, the correct play in the second example (cash the single honor first) is the opposite of that in the first layout (cash one of the double honors first). This demonstrates how difficult it is to memorize the right plays. You must train yourself to visualize the possible defensive holdings and work out which line of play will guard against them.

The opponents hold the queen

This combination is often misplayed:

♠ A K J 10 6 3

♠ 7 5

Time and again, you will see declarers cashing the ace (to pick up a single queen offside), before returning to the South hand to finesse the jack. Once in a while the queen will be singleton offside and they will reap an undeserved reward. Four times as often, however, East will hold a singleton nine, eight, four or two, and these declarers will go down. The correct play is to finesse on the first round, thereby picking up four of East's possible five singletons.

When you have three or more cards in the shorter holding, it is right to cash a high honor first:

◇ A K J 9 2

◇ 10 7 4

If you finesse on the first round you will lose an unnecessary trick to a singleton queen offside. Cash the ace first, to guard against this holding, and you will still be able to pick up an original queen fourth holding with West. (If West holds all five missing diamonds you cannot pick up the suit anyway).

This is a familiar holding:

◇ A J 10 2

◇ K 7 6 3

When the suit breaks 3-2, you can pick up the queen on either side. You should usually play the king first, rather than the ace, since this also allows you to score four tricks when West holds queen fourth or queen fifth. If East has these holdings you cannot score more than three tricks anyway. ('King first' gives you a 43% chance of netting four tricks. 'Ace first' reduces this to 30%.)

Sometimes the presence of spot-cards as low as the six and seven can affect the best play in a suit:

♣ A K 10 6

♣ J 5 3 2

Here you would play the ace first, then finesse dummy's ten. Leading the jack on the first round can never assist you and will cost you a trick when West holds a singleton queen.

Now let's give dummy the seven-spot:

♣ A K 10 7

♣ J 5 3 2

The best play now is to lead the jack! You lose out when West has a singleton queen, yes, but you gain when East holds a singleton nine or eight. The first round will go: jack, queen, ace, eight (say). East will show out on dummy's king and you can return to the South hand to finesse the seven.

The opponents hold the queen and ten

Suppose you need to play this familiar suit for four tricks:

♠ J 6 4

♠ A K 9 3 2

You start by cashing the ace, on which both defenders play low cards. Playing the king next will work fine when the suit breaks 3-2, even better when the queen comes down doubleton and you make five tricks in the suit. If either defender shows out on the second round though, you will fail in your objective to score four tricks. How can we do better?

The way to ensure only one loser is to cash the ace, then lead low towards dummy's jack. If the suit breaks 3-2, your king will collect the outstanding spades on the third round. What will happen when West holds four spades?

♠ J 6 4

♠ Q 10 8 5   N W E S   ♠ 7

♠ A K 9 3 2

No problem there. Your jack will score a trick on the second or third round, leaving West with just one trick.

What if East has four spades?

♠ J 6 4

♠ 7   N W E S   ♠ Q 10 8 5

♠ A K 9 3 2

West shows out on the second round and East captures dummy's jack with the queen. You can then enter dummy, in some other suit, and finesse against East's ten. Again, you lose only one trick.

Here is another old friend:

♠ A K J 5

♠ 7 4 2

When you need four tricks, you must finesse the jack and pray that West started with queen third. Should you need only three tricks to make the contract, a safety play is available. You should start by cashing the ace and king (annoying East if he started with queen doubleton). If the queen does not fall, you return to the South hand in another suit and lead towards the jack. You will score three tricks if West has the queen, if the suit breaks 3-3, or if East has a singleton or doubleton queen.

The safety play will cost you an overtrick when West has precisely queen third, but it will bump your chance of making the contract from 68% to 76%.

The opponents hold the queen and jack

What do you make of this combination:

♠ A 9 6 4 3

♠ K 10

You can never score all five tricks but what is the best chance for four? Any rational play will succeed when the suit breaks 3-3, so you should look at the 4-2 divisions. The easy winner is to play low to the ten. This succeeds whenever East holds Q-J-x-x (if he splits, your ten and nine will be equals against his remaining honor). It also succeeds when East holds a doubleton honor. The ten will lose to West's honor fourth, but the king will drop East's honor, leaving the dummy's cards high.

The next combination will set many groups of bridge players arguing:

♠ A 10 9 2

♠ K 7 5 2

Suppose you need a full four tricks from this combination. If West holds a singleton honor there is nothing you can do, so you start by cashing the king. Luck is with you and the jack (or queen) appears from East. What should you do next? Should you play a spade to the ace, hoping that East started with Q-J doubleton, or finesse the ten, playing for East's honor to be singleton?

The better chance, by the huge factor of almost 2:1, is to finesse the ten. The easiest way to understand why is to realize that these three East holdings are approximately equal in probability:

♠QJ   ♠Q   ♠J

If you always finesse when the queen or jack appears, you will win two times out three. This remains true, whichever honor any particular East player would choose to play from Q-J doubleton.

The concept behind this, and in many similar cases, is known as the 'Principle of Restricted Choice'. It is mathematically provable that it is more likely that a player was forced to play a particular card than that he chose to play it from equals. So, when East plays the jack (or queen) here, it is more likely it was a forced play, from a singleton, than a chosen card from Q-J doubleton.

Should you meet players who dispute the validity of Restricted Choice, on no account try to convert them. Their minds are set. You will be wasting your time! Meanwhile, you can continue to win two times out of three, whereas they will win only half as often.

Now suppose you need only three tricks, from this holding:

♠ A 9 7 2

♠ K 10 8 3

You must attempt to protect against a Q-J-x-x holding on one side or other. It would be too committal to cash an honor on the first round.

You must guess whether to finesse the ten or the nine.

Let's say you start with a low card towards the ten. If the queen or jack appears from East, you win with the ace. You are safe for three tricks and the best chance for four is to run the ten through West next. (Restricted Choice is at work again. East is roughly twice as likely to hold a singleton honor as Q-J doubleton).

Most of the time East will play low and the ten will lose to one or other honor with West. Which honor should you cash on the second round, do you think? You should cash the king. This will lose when West started with a singleton queen or jack, but win when East started with a singleton four, five or six. The odds are 3:2 in your favor.

When the suit in question is a side suit in a trump contract, your choice of play may be affected by the knowledge that West would probably have led the suit initially if he held a small singleton. You should finesse the nine on the first round, playing the king next if the finesse loses. Playing in this way, you will score three tricks against all seven of the remaining 4-1 breaks. (You discount as unlikely the three cases where West has a small singleton.)

The opponents hold the queen, jack and ten

Do you have a headache yet? To relieve it, let's look at the next combination in the context of a full deal:

```
Neither Vul.         ♠ 8 5 2
Dealer South         ♡ J 9 4 3
                     ◇ A 8
                     ♣ A K 4 3

♠ 10                              ♠ Q J 7 3
♡ Q 10 7 6 2         N            ♡ A K
◇ 6 5 3          W       E        ◇ Q J 10 7 4
♣ 10 8 5 2           S            ♣ 9 7

                     ♠ A K 9 6 4
                     ♡ 8 5
                     ◇ K 9 2
                     ♣ Q J 6
```

WEST	NORTH	EAST	SOUTH
			1♠
pass	2♣	pass	2♠
pass	4♠	all pass	

West leads the ♡6 against your spade game. East scores two tricks in the suit, then switches to the ◇Q. You win with the king, preserving the ace as a later entry to dummy, and cash the ace of trumps, the ten showing from West. What next?

The diamond loser can be discarded on dummy's fourth club, so everything depends on restricting your trump losers to one. If trumps break 3-2, any play will suffice. Equally, if West has played a humorous ten from Q-J-10-7 there is nothing you can do about it. What if East holds all three remaining trumps?

By playing a low spade to the eight now, you expose the bad trump split while you can still handle it. West wins the eight of trumps with the jack and returns a diamond to dummy's ace. You can then finesse against West's queen of trumps, draw his last trump, and cash your clubs to discard your diamond loser.

The opponents hold the king

When only the king is missing, it is generally right to finesse with ten cards or fewer between the hands. With eleven, you would normally play for the drop. However, you have a chance to insult the opponents in this situation:

```
                  ♠ Q 9 7 6 2
                 ┌─────────┐
                 │    N    │
        ♠ K      │ W     E │    ♠ 8 5
                 │    S    │
                 └─────────┘
                  ♠ A J 10 4 3
```

You lead the queen and East plays one of his small cards. If you judge that East is a weak enough player to cover when he holds a doubleton king (covering would be bad defense, of course), you can rise from with the ace. When West's king happens to be singleton, you will emerge triumphant.

The opponents hold the king and queen

How would you handle this common holding:

◇ A J 6 3

◇ 10 7 2

If you need three tricks, you would play low to the jack, succeeding when West holds K-Q or K-Q-x. More difficult perhaps is to determine the safest play for two tricks. What do you reckon?

As with many of these combinations, you should play the ace first, to guard against a singleton honor on either side. Next you must lead towards the honor in the shorter holding (here the ten). By doing so, and later leading towards the jack if necessary, you will pick up an initial K-Q-x-x on either side. Leading towards the jack on the second round would not be so good, failing to pick up K-Q-x-x with East.

This is a good moment to mention an important type of safety play, one that is frequently spurned.

◇ A

◇ J 10 7 6 5 2

How would you play this suit for only two losers? You will see many players leading the jack on the second round. This wastes a trick unnecessarily when an opponent wins with a doubleton honor. His partner will then score two further tricks in the suit. You should lead a low card on the second round. This is as good as anything when the suit breaks 3-3. The gain comes when a defender wins with a doubleton honor and your J-10 can then drive out the remaining honor.

The opponents hold the king and jack

The best play on the next type of combination varies according to the spot-cards held:

♠ Q 10 5 4 2

♠ A 3

If you need four tricks from this holding, you must hope that the defenders' spades divide 3-3 and that you can guess well. You should cash the ace, then lead a second spade towards dummy. If East started with ♠KJx you have no chance, while if West has this holding you cannot go wrong. If the honors are split, you will have to guess whether to play the queen or the ten.

Add the nine to the longer holding and it is no longer an even guess:

♠ Q 10 9 4 2

♠ A 3

Seeking four tricks, you cash the ace and lead towards dummy, only low spades appearing so far. If you play the ten you will succeed only when West holds J-x-x. Make the better play of the queen and you will prevail when West holds K-x-x, and also when East holds J-x. Note that playing the ten does not help you when East holds a doubleton king. You will still have to lose a second spade trick to West's jack.

The same reasoning applies here:

♠ 3

♠ A Q 10 9 4 2

Playing low to the queen is the best percentage play, as you will lose only one trick when West holds the doubleton jack. If you play low to the ten and force West's doubleton king, you will still have to lose a trick to East's jack fourth.

Returning to the original layout, we will now make the dummy's spades even stronger:

♠ Q 10 9 8 5

♠ A 3

Most players would not realize that the eight made any difference. They would cash the ace and lead low to dummy's queen. However, there is a slightly better, although rather strange-looking line of play. Try leading the queen from dummy on the first round of the suit! This picks up three of the important doubletons: J-x on either side or K-x with East. The other line picks up only the two J-x cases.

Let's imagine that you stumble upon this holding for the first time:

♠ A 10 4

♠ Q 6 5 3 2

You can't guarantee three tricks against a 5-0 split, but you can against all other breaks. How would you set about it?

Many people would plan to take two finesses. Perhaps they would lead the four towards the queen, intending to finesse the ten later if the queen lost to the king. That line is as good as any when you are trying to maximize your haul from the suit, but it does not guarantee three tricks against a 4-1 break; it will lose when West holds a singleton king. Perhaps it's better to finesse the ten first? No, that loses to a singleton jack with East. Only one line works against all the 4-1 breaks, and that is to take no finesses at all.

You should cash the ace first, guarding against all the layouts where a defender has a singleton honor. You must then cross to your hand in another suit and lead low towards dummy's ten. If West holds ♠KJ98, he will only be able to make two tricks because of the positional value of the ten behind him. If East has this holding, he can capture the ten with his jack, but you will later lead towards your queen, restricting him to two tricks.

The opponents hold the king and ten

How would you play this combination, to maximize your chance of scoring five tricks?

◇ J 8 6 3

◇ A Q 9 7 4

You should play a low card to the queen. This will produce five tricks when East holds a doubleton or singleton king. It will succeed also when West holds a singleton ten, since you can then return to dummy in some other suit and finesse against East's king. Many players take an unnecessary risk by leading the jack on the first round. When East has a singleton king, West will score an undeserved trick with the ten on the third round. The general guideline in these situations is: don't lead an honor for a finesse unless you can afford the card to be covered.

Suppose now that you hold ten cards between the hands:

◇ J 8 6 3 2

◇ A Q 9 7 4

What is the best chance of five tricks? Cashing the ace would win only when the king was singleton in either hand (about 26% of the time). Finessing against the king offers much better odds. However, it would be a mistake to lead low to the queen. Why? Because more than one time in ten (11% of the time to be precise), East will hold ◇ K 10 5. A finesse of the queen will succeed but you will still have to lose a trick to East's remaining king-ten.

It is a cost-nothing safety play to lead the jack from dummy to guard against this possibility. If East covers and West shows out, you can re-enter dummy in another suit and finesse against East's ten. You will make five tricks whenever East holds the king (a 50% chance, of course).

The opponents hold the king, jack and ten

We are on familiar territory with this holding:

◇ A Q 9 2

◇ 6 4 3

Needing three tricks, you should finesse the nine first in the hope that West holds both jack and ten. If the nine loses to the jack or ten, you finesse the queen next. You score three tricks when the suit breaks 3-3 and West holds the king or the jack-ten. You succeed also when West holds K-J-10-x or K-J-10-x-x.

Suppose now that you need only two diamond tricks. Would you play the same way?

It is still correct to play to the nine first. If this loses to the jack or ten however, you should cash the ace on the next round. This protects you against K-J or K-10 doubleton with East.

The next combination is more difficult but it is not impossible to work out the winning play. You just need to think along the right lines.

◇ Q 9 8 7 6

◇ A 4 3

How can you guarantee three tricks from this suit? You must look for a 100% play.

At the table, most players would start by cashing the ace of diamonds, or by playing a low diamond to the queen. Does either of those plays assure you of three tricks in the suit? No, if you lead low to the queen and it loses to a singleton king, West's J-10-5-2 will stop the suit twice more. Starting with the ace is even worse, since that loses when West is void or holds a singleton five or two.

Let's try something different — ducking the first round completely! Let's test this line of play against some unfavorable breaks.

$\Diamond$ Q 9 8 7 6

$\Diamond$ 2 $\begin{array}{c} N \\ W \quad E \\ S \end{array}$ $\Diamond$ K J 10 5

$\Diamond$ A 4 3

The first round is ducked to East's ten. On the second round we lead a low card from dummy, and let it run if East plays the five. Should this lose to West, the suit will have broken 3-2 and all will be well. If instead East plays the king or ten, we can win with the ace and drive out his remaining high card. So, we are safe if East has all the high diamonds. What if West holds them?

$\Diamond$ Q 9 8 7 6

$\Diamond$ K J 10 5 $\begin{array}{c} N \\ W \quad E \\ S \end{array}$ $\Diamond$ 2

$\Diamond$ A 4 3

The same line of play will produce three tricks here, too. If West plays the five on the first round, dummy's six will win the trick. If instead he plays the ten (or jack), dummy's queen will capture the trick and West will again make only two tricks.

What if the six loses to a singleton honor with East? That is no problem because when we lead a second round from dummy. East will show out. We can rise with the ace and lead back towards the queen.

It was hard work, but we were able to uncover a 100% safety play. The more times you perform such an exercise, the easier it will become.

The opponents hold the ace and king

How would you attempt to conjure two tricks from this holding?

♡ Q 7 6 2

♡ J 8 5 3

You start by leading towards one or other honor. If this is a side suit in a trump contract, West would often have led the suit when holding both the ace and king. So, begin with a low card from the dummy.

When East holds A-K-x, the play will be an immediate success. Most of the time the jack will lose to an honor with West. You should then duck the second round, gaining when East started with a doubleton honor.

Suppose that you need only one trick from the holding. Can you spot the 100% safety play? To avoid having an honor captured by a singleton honor, leaving the other defender with three more tricks in the suit, you must duck the first round. You can then guarantee a trick by leading towards either honor.

The opponents hold ace and queen

This is an important holding, familiar in the trump suit:

◇ K J 9 6 5

◇ 8 4 3 2

Seeking four tricks from the suit, you lead a low card towards dummy. West produces the ten or seven. Which card should you play? If someone whispered in your ear that West had started with a doubleton honor, it would be a 50-50 guess which card to choose. Without such inside information, the jack is a clear favorite. The 2-2 situations (A-x or Q-x with West) cancel out and the jack gains when West holds A-Q-7 or A-Q-10.

Newcomers to the game soon learn that there is little point in leading the queen when they hold Q-J-x opposite A-x-x-x. By leading towards the queen-jack, they can score three tricks when the king is well placed. The same idea applies here, too:

♣ K 6 5 2

♣ J 10 3

Needing two tricks from the suit, you should lead twice towards the jack-ten.

The opponents hold the ace and jack

Do you remember the discussion on A-J-10-x opposite K-x-x-x — that you could only pick up queen fourth on one side? This situation is very similar:

♡ K 10 9 3

♡ Q 6 4

By leading towards the queen on the first round, you will collect three tricks when West holds the jack, even if he has four cards in the suit. Leading to the king is nowhere near so successful when East holds the jack. If the king wins and you lead the ten on the second round (hoping that East holds J-x-x), you will fail in your objective when East holds J-x or J-x-x-x.

Take the nine away and it is still right to play first towards the unaccompanied honor:

♡ K 10 6 3

♡ Q 5 2

A first-round finesse of the ten might lose to a singleton jack or to A-J doubleton. Lead low towards the queen on the first round and you avoid this fate.

Suppose that the queen loses to West's ace. What next? Seeking three tricks from the suit, you would finesse the ten on the second round. However, when you need only two tricks you should cash the king instead, picking up a doubleton jack offside. If the jack fails to show, you return to the South hand and lead towards the ten.

When the ten lies in the shorter holding, however, it is best to finesse it on the first round:

♡ K 7 6 3

♡ Q 10 4

By playing low to the ten, then low to the queen, you score three tricks when East holds A-J, A-J-x, or J-x-x.

The opponents hold ace, queen and jack

When your only card of value is the king, the aim of any safety play will be to avoid losing it to the enemy ace.

♡ K 9 8 6 4 2

♡ 7 5 3

Needing five tricks, you lead towards the king. Needing only four tricks, you duck a round first — to guard against a singleton ace offside. When this is the trump suit, it is best tactically to lead the first round from dummy. If East holds something like A-10 doubleton, he may place you with the queen and rise with the ace to avoid some imagined end-play. The same applies when you have only eight cards between the hands.

Give yourself just seven cards, now:

◇ K 8 7 5

◇ 9 4 2

Needing two tricks, you duck a round (saving an extra undertrick when East has a singleton ace), then lead towards the king on the second round. You hope that the ace is onside and the suit breaks 3-3. If you required only one trick from the suit, you would duck two rounds before leading towards the king. This would safeguard against a doubleton ace with East. (You might as well lead the second round towards the king, in case West started with A-x-x and is tempted to play the ace on the second round.)

Key points

1. Some safety plays within a suit aim to avoid the loss of a trick to a singleton or doubleton honor offside. For example, if you need only three tricks from A-K-J-4 opposite 7-5-2 you cash the ace and king first, then lead towards the jack.

2. Other safety plays guard against a bad break. For example to guarantee four tricks from A-10-6-5-2 opposite K-9-7-3 you should finesse the ten (or the nine) on the first round.

A.

♣ A J 10 9 2

♣ 6 5 4 3

There are three reasonable ways to play this combination for
four tricks: (a) cashing the ace first, (b) finessing the jack, then
playing the ace if the finesse loses, and (c) taking two finesses.
Which is the best play? Which is the worst play?

B.

♠ A 9 6 3

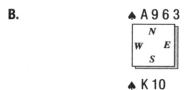

♠ K 10

How would you play this combination for three tricks?

C.

♡ J 6 5

$$
\begin{array}{c}
N \\
W \quad E \\
S
\end{array}
$$

♡ A 10 4 3 2

The best chance of making four tricks from this combination is
to play low to the ten (succeeding when East has K-Q-x or a
doubleton honor). Let's say you need only three tricks from the
suit. Is this still the right thing to do? If not, how should you
play?

D.

♣ 10 4 3

♣ A Q 6 5 2

Earlier, we discussed the best play for three tricks when holding A-10-4 opposite Q-6-5-3-2. Cashing the ace, then leading towards the ten, was the way to maximize your chances. How would you play for three tricks here?

E.

♠ 4 2

♠ A K 10 9 5 3

How would you play this combination for six tricks? Can you improve your chances if you need only five tricks from the suit?

F.

◇ J 4 2

◇ A 9 7 6 5 3

How would you play this diamond suit if you needed five tricks? Can you see a way to guarantee your contract when you need only four tricks from this suit?

Answers

A. (a) If you play the ace first, you score four tricks when the suit breaks 2-2 (40%), and also when it breaks 3-1 and an honor falls singleton (25%). That's a total of 65%. (b) If you take one finesse, playing the ace next if the finesse loses, you score four tricks when West holds K-Q-x-x (5%), when West holds K-Q-x (12.5%), when the suit breaks 2-2 (40%), and when West has a singleton honor (12.5%). That's a total of 70%, better than the first line. (c) If you take two finesses, you fail to score four tricks only when East holds both honors (24%). That makes it a 76% line — easily best!

B. You should finesse the ten on the first round. This will succeed when East holds both the missing honors, or one honor guarded fewer than three times. Suppose the cards lie like this, for example:

```
              ♠ A 9 6 3
                  N
  ♠ J 7 5 4    W     E    ♠ Q 8 2
                  S
              ♠ K 10
```

The ten loses to the jack but East's queen falls on the third round and dummy's nine produces a third trick. When West holds queen third or jack third, there is nothing you can do.

C. If you start by leading low to the ten, you will fail in this situation:

```
              ♡ J 6 5
                  N
    ♡ Q       W     E    ♡ K 9 8 7
                  S
              ♡ A 10 4 3 2
```

Similarly, low to the jack will fail when East holds a singleton honor. To ensure three tricks against anything except a 5-0 split, cash the ace and then lead low towards the jack.

D. The two holdings are exactly the same and again you should cash the ace, then lead towards the ten. This will produce three tricks against any distribution except a 5-0 break. Similar combinations often come in different guises. You can see that once you cash the ace, this combination is the same as the earlier one.

E. The best chance of making six tricks is to lead from dummy, intending to play the ten. If East plays an honor, win and re-enter dummy in another suit and again lead towards your hand, intending to finesse. This produces six tricks when East began with ♠QJ or ♠QJx (13% of the time). You will make five tricks 82% of the time. When only five tricks are required, you can bump this figure to almost 88% by cashing a high honor first. This play gains over 'two finesses' when West holds Q-J doubleton and an honor falls. (Since you cannot then pick up an initial honor fourth with East, you will continue with the king, in fact scoring all six tricks.) When no honor falls under the ace, cross to dummy and lead towards your hand intending to play the ten. You will still succeed when East holds the Q-J-x-x.

F. Needing five tricks from this holding, you should cash the ace, then lead towards the jack. You will make five tricks when the suit divides 2-2 or East holds a singleton queen or king. By following this line you will make five tricks 53% of the time, but only three tricks when the suit breaks 4-0. To guarantee four tricks against any distribution, you must lead towards the jack on the first round. If East is void, then the positional value of dummy's jack ensures that West's ◇KQ108 is worth only two tricks. If West shows out on the first round, you can lead twice towards your ace-nine, restricting East to two tricks in the suit.

Full Hand Safety Plays

Counting your tricks is an integral part of sound declarer play. The safety play of a single suit would have little meaning if you had not already asked, and answered, the question, 'How many tricks do I need from this suit?' In other words, the play of a suit must be considered in the context of the full deal.

Declarer can guarantee his contract on our first hand, but many players would go down simply because they failed to count their tricks. If you have your counting boots on, cover the defenders' hands here:

```
Neither Vul.          ♠ 10 9
Dealer South          ♡ A 9 5 2
                      ◇ 3
                      ♣ A K 9 7 5 4
♠ K J 8 6 3 2                         ♠ 7 4
♡ Q J 7          ┌─────────┐          ♡ K 10 4
◇ —             │    N    │          ◇ J 9 7 6 5
♣ Q 6 3 2       │ W    E  │          ♣ J 10 8
                │    S    │
                └─────────┘
                      ♠ A Q 5
                      ♡ 8 6 3
                      ◇ A K Q 10 8 4 2
                      ♣ —
```

WEST	NORTH	EAST	SOUTH
			1◇
2♠	3♣	pass	3NT
all pass			

West leads the ♡Q. How would you play the contract?

If the diamond suit breaks 3-2 (or the jack is singleton), you will have seven diamonds, two clubs, one spade and one heart, a total of eleven tricks. Even if diamonds are 4-1, you can afford to lose a trick in that suit and still prevail. It is easy to become complacent in such circumstances.

Let's go back and count those tricks again — one spade, one heart and one club. You cannot afford to cash both club winners while in dummy, since this will establish too many tricks for the defenders if you subsequently have to give up a diamond trick. So, with three aces in the other suits, you need to play diamonds for six tricks. That doesn't look too tough, provided you realize it soon enough.

Let's say you win the ace of hearts at Trick 1. You then play off the ace of clubs, discarding a major-suit loser, and play a diamond. When East follows, you are home — provided you put in the ten of diamonds! If this loses to the jack, the most the defense will be able to take is three heart tricks. When you regain the lead, you will have one spade and six diamonds to go with the two tricks already made. On the actual deal West will discard on the ten of diamonds. You can then concede a diamond trick to East and claim the contract.

There is no recovery if you play a top diamond on the first round. You would then need to concede two diamond tricks to set up the suit and the defenders would beat you to the finish line.

Discovery play

Sometimes you cannot tell at the outset how many tricks are needed from the key suit. You must perform some detective work first. Back in Chapter 1, we saw how you could use a safety play to guarantee three tricks from the club suit in the next deal. Is this deal an appropriate setting for such a safety play, do you think?

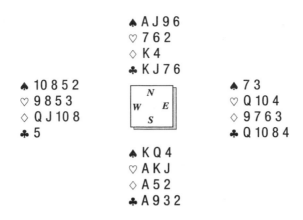

♠ A J 9 6
♡ 7 6 2
◇ K 4
♣ K J 7 6

♠ 10 8 5 2
♡ 9 8 5 3
◇ Q J 10 8
♣ 5

♠ 7 3
♡ Q 10 4
◇ 9 7 6 3
♣ Q 10 8 4

♠ K Q 4
♡ A K J
◇ A 5 2
♣ A 9 3 2

How would you play 6NT after West leads the ◇Q?

To decide how to play the clubs, you must know how many tricks the other three suits will yield. This is not simply a matter of counting tricks, because you do not yet know how many heart tricks you have. You must find out! After winning the diamond lead with the king, you finesse the ♡J, a 'discovery play'. Here the finesse will succeed and you can then count nine tricks outside clubs. With only three more tricks required from the club suit, you will make the appropriate safety play — king first, then a small club to the nine. Had the heart finesse lost, you would have been forced to play the club suit for four tricks. (Do you remember the right play? Low to the jack, to cater for a singleton queen with West.)

Comparing two chances

In general, we have been sparing with our use of percentages in this book. They are not everyone's cup of tea and we wanted to avoid critical letters of the type 'On page 27, I think you will find that your 57.2% figure should be 57.9%. You did not allow for...'.

Nevertheless, it is useful to know the basic probabilities associated with finesses and the various breaks in a suit. They can help you to calculate the best safety play in a single suit, and also to compare two different options within a whole hand.

We will look at finesses first:

AQ6

852

A simple finesse of a queen is 50%, always assuming that there is no enemy bidding that might affect the odds.

AQ10

763

In this example, you play low to the ten, then low to the queen. In rough figures, there is a 24% chance that both honors will be onside (giving you three tricks), and a 24% chance that both honors will be offside (giving you just one trick). The remaining 52% of the time, one finesse will lose and the other will win — you will score two tricks.

AJ10

954

By finessing twice here, unlike the previous example, you will score a second trick 76% of the time, failing only when East holds both the two missing honors.

Now for the more common breaks in a suit.

CARDS	BREAK	ODDS	CARDS	BREAK	ODDS
4	4-0	10%	6	6-0	1%
	3-1	41%		5-1	15%
	2-2	49%		4-2	48%
				3-3	36%
5	5-0	4%			
	4-1	28%			
	3-2	68%			

With this ready reckoner at your elbow, what is the safest way to play this 3NT contract?

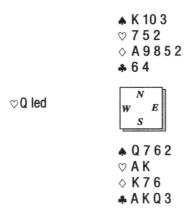

♠ K 10 3
♡ 7 5 2
◇ A 9 8 5 2
♣ 6 4

♡Q led

♠ Q 7 6 2
♡ A K
◇ K 7 6
♣ A K Q 3

You have seven tricks on top and two extra winners might come from either the spades or the diamonds. Should you duck a diamond, playing to set up that suit, or finesse the ♠10, hoping that West holds the jack?

The diamond play will succeed when the suit breaks 3-2, which is (see previous page) a 68% chance. Finessing the ♠10 is only a 50% chance, so the safer play is to duck a diamond. In fact, playing on diamonds is easily superior because you can cash the king, planning to duck the second round. If West shows out on the second diamond, you can change course — rising with dummy's ace and playing a spade to the queen. Now try this 6NT contract:

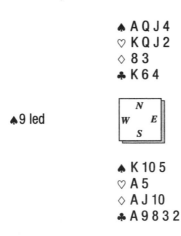

♠ A Q J 4
♡ K Q J 2
◇ 8 3
♣ K 6 4

♠9 led

♠ K 10 5
♡ A 5
◇ A J 10
♣ A 9 8 3 2

You have eleven top tricks. Should you attempt a twelfth in

diamonds, taking two finesses? Or is it better to play on clubs, hoping for a 3-2 break?

The chance of one or both diamond honors being onside is 76%. Against that, the chance of a 3-2 club break is 68%. So the diamonds have it. Or do they? Suppose you start by cashing the ace and king of clubs, rather than ducking a club. If the suit breaks 3-2, you will simply give up a club. If the clubs break 4-1, a fair chunk of your chances in the diamond suit will still be alive. If it is East who holds the club length, the diamond finesses will be into the safe hand and you will succeed if the diamond honors are split. Even if it is West who holds the club length, you will still succeed when East holds both honors. So, testing the club suit first is in fact safer than playing on diamonds. Your total prospects are well over 80%.

Combining two chances

The last hand in the previous section leads us neatly to a new topic — how to combine the chances offered by two different suits, rather than putting all your money on just one of them. The next hand is not really difficult but would often be misplayed.

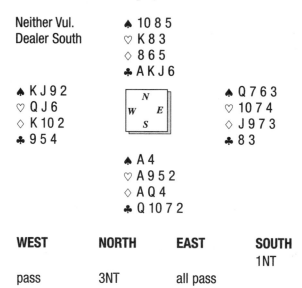

Neither Vul.
Dealer South

North:
♠ 10 8 5
♡ K 8 3
◇ 8 6 5
♣ A K J 6

West:
♠ K J 9 2
♡ Q J 6
◇ K 10 2
♣ 9 5 4

East:
♠ Q 7 6 3
♡ 10 7 4
◇ J 9 7 3
♣ 8 3

South:
♠ A 4
♡ A 9 5 2
◇ A Q 4
♣ Q 10 7 2

WEST	NORTH	EAST	SOUTH
			1NT
pass	3NT	all pass	

West leads a fourth-best ♠2 against your 3NT contract. You allow East's queen to win and capture the ♠3 return with the ace. What next?

There are eight top tricks and many players would look no further than the diamond finesse in their quest for a ninth. Half the time they would draw an undeserved 'Well played, partner' from across the table. Not on this occasion.

The opening lead of the ♠2, backed up by East's ♠3 return, has announced to the world that spades are 4-4. It is therefore safe to duck a round of hearts, possibly setting up a winner in that suit. It's true that the diamond finesse, on its own, is a better prospect than finding the hearts 3-3. But, there may be no need to rely on just one of these chances. If the defenders win the heart and cash their two spade tricks, ending in the West hand, you will have time to test for a 3-3 heart break before falling back on the diamond finesse. In other words, you will able to combine your chances in hearts and diamonds.

Expert defenders would aim to thwart you on this type of deal, by playing a diamond through your tenace before you have been able to test the heart suit. On the present layout you can prevent this by ensuring that you duck the heart to West rather than East. Lead a small heart first from hand; if West inserts an honor on the first round of hearts, you will duck. If he plays low, you will win with dummy's king and duck the second round to West.

Does anything else occur to you on the deal? Since you are not reliant on the entries provided by the club suit, you should cash that suit first, before ducking a heart. A defender with four hearts might decide to throw one away.

Sometimes you can combine playing for the drop in one suit with a finesse in another. You must calculate which suit gives you the better chance of dropping the missing honor. Look at this deal:

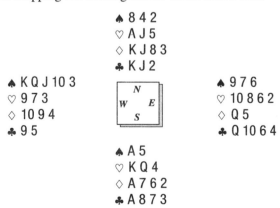

           ♠ 8 4 2
           ♡ A J 5
           ◇ K J 8 3
           ♣ K J 2

♠ K Q J 10 3   ♠ 9 7 6
♡ 9 7 3   ♡ 10 8 6 2
◇ 10 9 4   ◇ Q 5
♣ 9 5   ♣ Q 10 6 4

           ♠ A 5
           ♡ K Q 4
           ◇ A 7 6 2
           ♣ A 8 7 3

West leads the ♠K against 3NT. You win the second round and can count eight top tricks. There is an apparent choice of minor-suit finesses? However, it would be poor play to take an immediate finesse. A better idea is to try to drop one of the minor-suit queens before falling back on a finesse in the other suit. Since you hold eight cards in diamonds and only seven in clubs, the diamond queen is more likely to be doubleton than the club queen. You cash the ace and king of diamonds and are rewarded on this occasion when the queen falls from East. Had the queen not appeared, you would have taken the club finesse.

On the next deal West leads the ♠10 against 6NT. You have a choice of finesses to take. Which do you think offers the better chance?

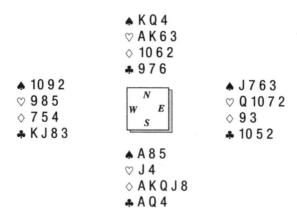

```
              ♠ K Q 4
              ♡ A K 6 3
              ◇ 10 6 2
              ♣ 9 7 6
♠ 10 9 2                      ♠ J 7 6 3
♡ 9 8 5        N             ♡ Q 10 7 2
◇ 7 5 4     W     E          ◇ 9 3
♣ K J 8 3      S             ♣ 10 5 2
              ♠ A 8 5
              ♡ J 4
              ◇ A K Q J 8
              ♣ A Q 4
```

There are eleven top tricks and a successful club finesse will bring your total to twelve. Is there any other chance? Yes, a heart towards the jack would land a twelfth trick if East held the heart queen. Can you see any reason to favor one finesse rather than the other?

It's not close, really! After winning the spade lead, you should play a heart to the jack. If this loses, you can still take the club finesse. You will succeed if either finesse is right. Suppose you take the club finesse first and it fails. With one trick already lost, it is no longer possible to lead towards the heart jack.

Safety plays to retain entries in a single suit

Sometimes a safety play is required to avoid a potential entry problem. Suppose you are blessed with this diamond combination:

◇ A K Q 7 3

◇ 5 2

Looking at the suit in isolation, you would cash the top honors. If the suit divided 3-3, you would score all five tricks. If it broke 4-2, you would concede a fourth round of the suit and later enjoy the long card. Suppose this is the full deal, though:

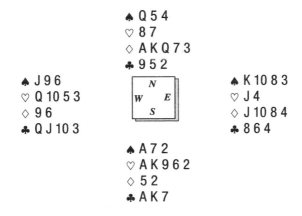

♠ Q 5 4
♡ 8 7
◇ A K Q 7 3
♣ 9 5 2

♠ J 9 6
♡ Q 10 5 3
◇ 9 6
♣ Q J 10 3

♠ K 10 8 3
♡ J 4
◇ J 10 8 4
♣ 8 6 4

♠ A 7 2
♡ A K 9 6 2
◇ 5 2
♣ A K 7

West leads the ♣Q against 3NT. There would be little purpose in a hold-up, and a spade switch would be unwelcome, so you win with the ace. What now? You have eight top tricks. If you play diamonds from the top, discovering they are not 3-3, you will go down. You can concede a diamond to East, but the ♠Q will not provide an entry back to dummy. If instead you duck a heart, you will find that this suit fails to break 3-3 too.

A safety play against a 4-2 diamond break is required. You must duck the first round of diamonds. You can then win the return and enjoy four diamond tricks (unless the suit breaks 5-1).

The next hand features a similar play in a slightly different guise.

If you feel up to a test, cover the East-West hands and be declarer.

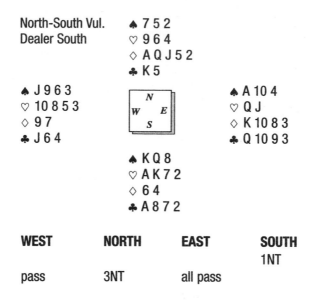

North-South Vul.
Dealer South

North:
♠ 7 5 2
♡ 9 6 4
◇ A Q J 5 2
♣ K 5

West:
♠ J 9 6 3
♡ 10 8 5 3
◇ 9 7
♣ J 6 4

East:
♠ A 10 4
♡ Q J
◇ K 10 8 3
♣ Q 10 9 3

South:
♠ K Q 8
♡ A K 7 2
◇ 6 4
♣ A 8 7 2

WEST	NORTH	EAST	SOUTH
			1NT
pass	3NT	all pass	

West leads the ♠3 to his partner's ace and East returns the ♠10. What is your plan?

The defenders could have made life tougher for you, but you must still be alert to take full advantage. Counting your tricks, you can see two each in spades, hearts and clubs. Therefore, you need three diamond tricks to fulfill your contract.

If you play a diamond to the jack, that will be the end of your chances. Provided East is awake, he will allow the jack of diamonds to hold. Perhaps you re-enter your hand in hearts and repeat the diamond finesse. East wins with the king and, with only one outside entry to dummy (the ♣K), you will score just two diamond tricks. One down. See what a difference it makes if, at Trick 3, you play a low diamond from both your own hand and dummy. Let's say that East wins and returns his third spade. Now, you can play a diamond to the jack. It no longer helps East to duck his king, as you can easily establish the fifth diamond while the king of clubs remains as an entry. By ducking the first diamond you give up all hope of scoring five diamond tricks, but this is a small price to pay for ensuring your contract.

As it happens, East could have beaten the contract by switching to clubs at Trick 2. When dummy possesses a strong suit, it is often good tactics for the defenders to attack dummy's outside entries.

Repeating a 'successful' finesse

Suppose you hold some combination headed by the A-Q-J and take a successful finesse in the suit. Should you repeat the finesse? It depends on whether you can afford the second finesse to lose. Always bear in mind that the defender sitting over the holding may have held up on the first round. Look at the fate declarer suffered here:

North-South Vul.
Dealer South

♠ 8 3
♡ 9 6 2
◇ 5
♣ A Q J 8 7 3 2

♠ Q J 10 7 6
♡ 10 5 3
◇ Q 7 3
♣ 10 5

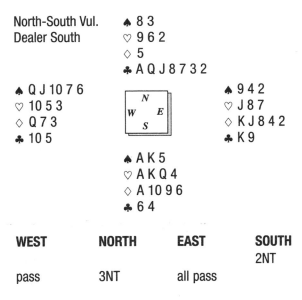

♠ 9 4 2
♡ J 8 7
◇ K J 8 4 2
♣ K 9

♠ A K 5
♡ A K Q 4
◇ A 10 9 6
♣ 6 4

WEST	NORTH	EAST	SOUTH
			2NT
pass	3NT	all pass	

West led the ♠Q against 3NT, declarer winning with the ace. A club to dummy's queen won the next trick, since East could see that there was no future for the defense if he took the king. Declarer returned to hand with the ace of hearts and led another club. When the ten appeared from West, declarer reached with some confidence for dummy's jack. Disillusionment was swift. East won with the bare king and cleared the spade suit. Even though the hearts broke 3-3, only eight tricks were available.

How could South have avoided this humiliating experience? After all, West might well have held ♣K105. Before repeating the club finesse, declarer should have tested the heart suit. When it divided 3-3, he would have been able to count nine top tricks: two spades, four hearts, one diamond and two clubs. By restricting his ambitions to the nine tricks needed for the contract and rising with the club ace on the second round, declarer would in fact have ended with all thirteen tricks!

Safety plays involving a two-way finesse

Suppose you are faced with a suit like this:

◊ A K 9 3

◊ Q 10 6 4

You cash the ace and two small cards appear. Either defender could still hold J-x-x and it is a guess which honor to play next. Some declarers will look at the spot-cards produced by the defenders on the first round. If West played the two and East the eight, they may conclude that West is more likely to hold four diamonds. A good defender may well play a deceptive eight from J-8-6-5, though, so this is a not a reliable guide in good company.

It is more likely that a grander view of the whole hand will point you to the best play in the suit. Sometimes a count, or partial count, of the other suits will indicate that only one defender has room for four diamonds. On the following deal, the indication is different.

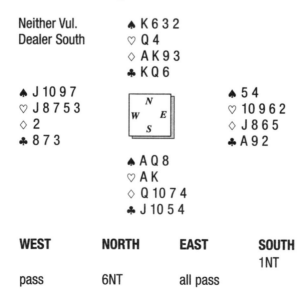

Neither Vul.
Dealer South

♠ K 6 3 2
♡ Q 4
◊ A K 9 3
♣ K Q 6

♠ J 10 9 7
♡ J 8 7 5 3
◊ 2
♣ 8 7 3

♠ 5 4
♡ 10 9 6 2
◊ J 8 6 5
♣ A 9 2

♠ A Q 8
♡ A K
◊ Q 10 7 4
♣ J 10 5 4

WEST	NORTH	EAST	SOUTH
			1NT
pass	6NT	all pass	

West leads the ♠J, suggesting that he may hold length in the suit.

You win with the ace and knock out the ace of clubs. You can now count eleven top tricks and a successful view in diamonds will bring you a twelfth. Both defenders follow low to the ace of diamonds. Which diamond honor will you cash next?

You should cash the diamond king next. As it happens, West shows out and a marked finesse against East's ◇J lands the slam. Why was it right to play East for the diamond length? One guideline was that you expected West to be longer than East in spades, so East was more likely to be longer in diamonds. However, this was not the main reason. By playing diamonds in this way, you were likely to make the contract, whichever defender held four diamonds! If the diamond length were with West, he would be squeezed in diamonds and spades when you cashed your winners in the other two suits.

Key points

1. The best play within a single suit may be affected by a grander view of the whole hand. For example, you may need to keep a particular defender off lead.

2. Combining chances in two different suits will usually be better than relying on just one chance.

A.

♠ A 5
♡ Q J 7
◇ Q J 8 2
♣ A K J 4

♡6 led

```
      N
  W       E
      S
```

♠ Q 9 6 3
♡ A K 9 5
◇ A K 6
♣ 7 3

West leads the ♡6 against your contract of 6NT. How will you play the contract?

B.

♠ A 7 4
♡ A 9 2
◇ A K J 3
♣ A 6 5

♡J led

```
      N
  W       E
      S
```

♠ K J 3
♡ K 6 4
◇ 8 7 2
♣ K Q J 3

Continuing to hold good cards, you reach 6NT again. West leads the ♡J. How will you play the contract?

C.

     ♠ Q 10 7 4
     ♡ A Q 9 7 6
     ◇ A 7
     ♣ A J

◇ Q led

```
      N
  W       E
      S
```

     ♠ A 6
     ♡ 4 2
     ◇ K 8 2
     ♣ Q 10 7 6 4 3

West leads the ◇ Q against your 3NT. How do you play the hand for maximum safety?

D.

     ♠ A K 5 3
     ♡ K 2
     ◇ K 6 3
     ♣ A 10 8 6

♠ Q led

```
      N
  W       E
      S
```

     ♠ 10
     ♡ A Q 10 8 7 6 4
     ◇ A 9 7 2
     ♣ 7

WEST	NORTH	EAST	SOUTH
3♠	3NT	pass	6♡
all pass			

West leads the queen of spades. Plan the play.

Answers

A. You have eleven top tricks and possibilities of a twelfth in both spades and clubs. To combine these two chances, you must play on spades first. Win the heart lead in dummy and lead a low spade to the queen. If this loses to West's king, you will win the return, cash the club ace (just in case the queen is singleton), then finesse the ♣J.

B. There is a possible safety play, to score three tricks in diamonds. By cashing the ace and king of diamonds, then leading towards the jack, you can catch queen doubleton with East (and still make three tricks if West holds the queen, or the suit breaks 3-3). To see whether you can afford this safety play, you must make a discovery play in spades, finessing the jack. If the spade finesse wins, go ahead with the safety play in diamonds. If the spade finesse loses, you will cash the diamond ace (saving a second undertrick when East holds a single queen), then take a normal finesse of the ◇J. If West holds queen third, you will score four tricks from the suit.

C. Five club tricks will bring your total to nine. You should win the diamond lead with the ace, then continue with the ace and jack of clubs. Even if the jack wins and the clubs break 4-1, you will be safe. You can cross to the ♠A and clear the club suit, later returning to the ◇K to enjoy the remaining clubs.

D. Ask yourself: What can go wrong? If East has all four trumps, you can easily pick them up. West will show out when you play a trump to the king and you can then finesse the ten. It is barely possible that West can hold all four trumps after his preempt, so what other risk is there? West may have an eight-card spade suit! If you play the ace or king of spades at Trick 1, East will ruff and you will go one down. To counter this, you should allow the ♠Q to win. You can then capture the return, draw trumps, and eventually throw two diamonds on dummy's ♠AK

CHAPTER 4

Safety Plays with Trumps

The presence of a trump suit adds additional elements to the mix. In this chapter we examine safety plays in the trump suit itself, and those involving side suits.

Some safety plays aim to ensure you maintain control of the hand. This is a common situation:

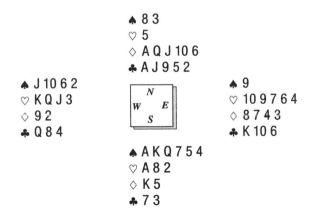

```
              ♠ 8 3
              ♡ 5
              ◇ A Q J 10 6
              ♣ A J 9 5 2
♠ J 10 6 2                    ♠ 9
♡ K Q J 3          N          ♡ 10 9 7 6 4
◇ 9 2          W       E      ◇ 8 7 4 3
♣ Q 8 4            S          ♣ K 10 6
              ♠ A K Q 7 5 4
              ♡ A 8 2
              ◇ K 5
              ♣ 7 3
```

You bid competently to six spades and West leads the ♡K, won with the ace. How will you attempt to make the slam?

If trumps break 3-2 there will be thirteen top tricks, so turn your mind to what will happen if the trumps break 4-1. Suppose you play two top trumps and one of the defenders shows out on the second round. You will then go down unless the defender with the long trumps has four diamonds (unlikely) and you can discard three losers in time.

What else can you try? There is no future in ruffing both your hearts because, after taking the second ruff, you will be stuck in dummy.

Since the contract is six spades rather than seven spades, you can afford to lose a trump trick. Try ducking a round of trumps at Trick 2. Barring some freak ruff in a minor, your contract will then be safe. The trump trick you could afford to lose was conceded at a safe moment — when dummy still had a trump to protect against a heart continuation.

The same principle applies on this slightly different deal:

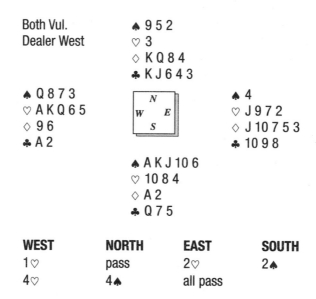

Both Vul.
Dealer West

North hand:
♠ 9 5 2
♡ 3
◇ K Q 8 4
♣ K J 6 4 3

West hand:
♠ Q 8 7 3
♡ A K Q 6 5
◇ 9 6
♣ A 2

East hand:
♠ 4
♡ J 9 7 2
◇ J 10 7 5 3
♣ 10 9 8

South hand:
♠ A K J 10 6
♡ 10 8 4
◇ A 2
♣ Q 7 5

WEST	NORTH	EAST	SOUTH
1♡	pass	2♡	2♠
4♡	4♠	all pass	

West leads the king of hearts and continues with the queen, which you ruff in dummy. How do you play?

We all hate to lose tricks to singleton honors, so perhaps you cross to the ace of spades, return to dummy with a high diamond, and play a second spade, intending to take the trump finesse. It is a rude awakening when East shows out. Not only will you have a second heart to lose when West gets in with his queen of trumps, you will also lose control. From this point, you will do well to make even nine tricks.

Let's go back to Trick 3. This time, you cross to the ace of diamonds and ruff your remaining heart loser. You then take the trump finesse. It loses, but this seems to be okay. West plays a fourth round of hearts and you ruff in hand. You continue to draw trumps, but when East shows out on the second round, you realize that West has as many trumps left as you. You have two choices, both of them bad. If you draw all of West's trumps, he will be able to cash a heart when he takes the ♣A. If instead you play on clubs before drawing West's trumps, he will force you with his fifth heart, establishing a second trump trick to go with his two aces. Either way, you will be one down.

Now try simply taking a spade finesse at Trick 3! What can West do? If he wins, a third heart will be unproductive as dummy can still ruff. If he returns a trump, he has given up the tempo to force your long trump. Finally, if West ducks his queen of spades, you simply ruff your third heart, play a diamond to the ace, cash the ace-king of trumps, and play a club. You will have ten easy tricks.

What was the lesson of these hands? When you can afford to lose a trump trick, do so when the defenders have the least chance to do any damage.

Safety plays to avoid a ruff

When the defenders lead a short suit against your trump contract, you will often have to adopt an unusual line of play in the trump suit to avoid a potential ruff. It's not too difficult here:

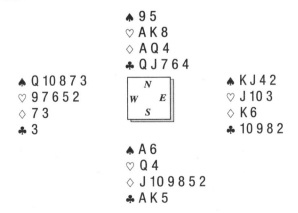

            ♠ 9 5
            ♡ A K 8
            ◇ A Q 4
            ♣ Q J 7 6 4

♠ Q 10 8 7 3   ♠ K J 4 2
♡ 9 7 6 5 2   ♡ J 10 3
◇ 7 3   ◇ K 6
♣ 3   ♣ 10 9 8 2

            ♠ A 6
            ♡ Q 4
            ◇ J 10 9 8 5 2
            ♣ A K 5

You bid (impressively, of course) to a small slam in diamonds and West leads the ♣3. As you can see, if you win in hand and take a trump finesse, East will win with the king and promptly give his partner a club ruff to defeat the slam.

Finessing in trumps presents an unnecessary risk. You can afford to lose one trump trick, but not two. Playing a trump to the ace and then a second round of trumps guarantees your contract.

Safety plays to establish a side suit

The danger is less apparent on the next deal and the vast majority of players would misplay it. If you would like to prove yourself, cover the East-West cards and take the hot seat in four hearts here:

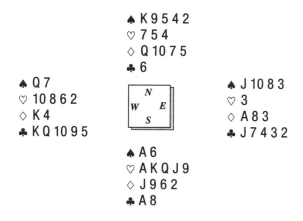

```
              ♠ K 9 5 4 2
              ♡ 7 5 4
              ◇ Q 10 7 5
              ♣ 6
   ♠ Q 7                    ♠ J 10 8 3
   ♡ 10 8 6 2       N       ♡ 3
   ◇ K 4        W       E   ◇ A 8 3
   ♣ K Q 10 9 5      S       ♣ J 7 4 3 2
              ♠ A 6
              ♡ A K Q J 9
              ◇ J 9 6 2
              ♣ A 8
```

West leads the ♣K. How do you play?

Suppose you win with the ace of clubs, ruff a club, and start to draw trumps. East will show out on the second round and it will be too late to sit back in your chair, wondering what to do about it. Whether or not you draw all the trumps first, the defenders will play clubs each time they take a diamond honor. You will lose control.

Instead you should win the ace of clubs and immediately play on diamonds. Yes, the defenders may now get a diamond ruff, but you will still make ten tricks. They can do nothing to threaten the contract because dummy's trumps protect you against club leads. (If the defenders switch elsewhere, you will eventually take a club ruff yourself before drawing trumps.)

On the deals so far in this chapter, you maintained control by conceding your potential loser(s) whilst dummy retained a trump. On the next deal, you must manage your trumps in such a way that you can overcome a bad break in your side suit. At the same time, you will also

have to take a safety play in the side suit itself. Okay, we've given you
a couple of clues. Cover the defenders' hands and take the South cards:

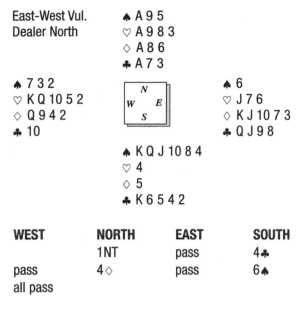

East-West Vul.
Dealer North

North: ♠ A 9 5 ♡ A 9 8 3 ◇ A 8 6 ♣ A 7 3

West: ♠ 7 3 2 ♡ K Q 10 5 2 ◇ Q 9 4 2 ♣ 10

East: ♠ 6 ♡ J 7 6 ◇ K J 10 7 3 ♣ Q J 9 8

South: ♠ K Q J 10 8 4 ♡ 4 ◇ 5 ♣ K 6 5 4 2

WEST	NORTH	EAST	SOUTH
	1NT	pass	4♣
pass	4◇	pass	6♠
all pass			

North opens a 15-17 1NT and a rare outing for the Gerber conven-
tion (4◇ showed zero or four aces) carries you to the slam. West leads
the king of hearts. How do you plan the play?

You win the ace of hearts and play the ace and king of trumps, East
discarding a diamond on the second round. If the clubs are divided 3-2,
you can just draw the last trump and claim, but what if they are 4-1?
Can you see a way to survive the poor break in both black suits?

There is no rush to draw the last trump. (By doing so, you would
be relying on a 3-2 club break anyway, so cashing the top clubs first
cannot cost.) If West has four clubs to go with the long trumps you cannot do anything about it — he will win the third round of clubs and
remove dummy's last trump, leaving you with a second club loser.
What if he has a singleton club, though?

Your aim is to cash two clubs, concede the third round of the suit,
then ruff the fourth round. Since you cannot afford to have a club honor
ruffed, you must lead the second round of clubs through the defender
with the missing trump. You cash the king of clubs and lead a second
round towards dummy. What can West do? If he ruffs in front of
dummy, then you will later be able to establish the clubs with a ruff. If

West refuses to ruff, you can win the ace of clubs and concede a club trick to East. Since East cannot play a trump, you will be able to ruff a club with dummy's last trump. You can then return to your hand to draw West's last trump.

If East had started with three trumps, the same strategy would have worked. In that case, you would have cashed the ace of clubs first, then led the second round of the suit through him.

Safety plays within the trump suit

Suppose this is your trump suit:

♠ A 8 6 3

♠ K J 7 4 2

You cash the ace and play a second trump, East playing the ten. Should you finesse or not? The odds slightly favor playing for the drop; however, by finessing the jack you may safeguard your contract by keeping East (the danger hand, we will imagine) off lead. Sometimes a finesse acts as a safety play because the trumps will be breaking 2-2 if it loses. This is the type of deal we have in mind:

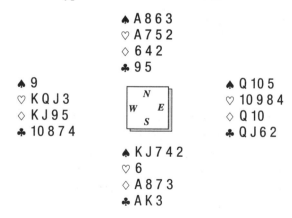

You arrive in four spades and win the heart lead in dummy. If your next move is to draw two rounds of trumps with the ace and king, you will go down. East will gain the lead in diamonds and will draw a third round of trumps. Unable to ruff a club and a diamond in the dummy, you will be defeated by the 4-2 diamond break.

Now try cashing the ace of trumps and continuing with a finesse of the jack. The contract is guaranteed. If the finesse loses, trumps will be 2-2 and you will be able to score the two ruffs you need. If the finesse wins, as here, you will not lose a trump trick and can afford one more loser in the minors.

On hands that present a potential finesse in the trump suit, ask yourself: 'Can I afford it if the finesse loses?' On the next deal the answer is 'Yes', for an unusual reason.

North-South Vul. ♠ 8 6 2
Dealer South   ♡ 7 3 2
                 ♢ A 7
                 ♣ K Q 8 6 3

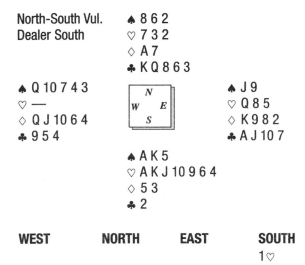

♠ Q 10 7 4 3   ♠ J 9
♡ —   ♡ Q 8 5
♢ Q J 10 6 4   ♢ K 9 8 2
♣ 9 5 4   ♣ A J 10 7

                 ♠ A K 5
                 ♡ A K J 10 9 6 4
                 ♢ 5 3
                 ♣ 2

WEST	NORTH	EAST	SOUTH
			1♡
pass	1NT	pass	4♡
all pass			

West leads the ♢ Q against your heart game and you win with dummy's ace. If trumps break 2-1 an easy overtrick beckons. After drawing trumps in two rounds, you will be able to set up a club trick. A third round of trumps to dummy's seven will serve as an entry and you can then discard your spade loser on the good club.

Suppose you give the matter no further thought and play a trump to the ace. You will go down! West will show out and you will lose a trick in every suit. You will have no real excuse. Once East followed to the first round of trumps, the contract could be guaranteed by finessing the jack of trumps. If West wins, you will have lost an unnecessary trump trick but you will still make the contract. With trumps known to be 2-1, you can use dummy's ♡7 as an entry to reach your club trick. When the cards lie as in the diagram, the finesse will gain directly — you will not lose a trump trick.

The cost of this safety play is that you lose your overtrick whenever West started with a singleton or doubleton queen of hearts. You will make ten tricks whenever East holds all three missing trumps though — something that will happen more than one time in ten. Call us high-powered salesmen, but this seems like a small premium to pay for such a worthwhile insurance policy.

There's no justice!

Over your bridge-playing career, safety plays will bring in IMPs, matchpoints, pounds, dollars, whatever, by the bushel. Bridge is not always a fair game, though, and now and again you will end with egg on your face. That's what happened on this deal from a British Premier League match:

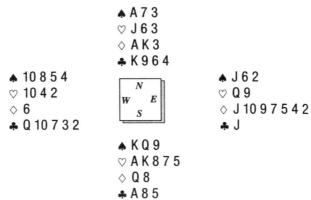

```
              ♠ A 7 3
              ♡ J 6 3
              ◇ A K 3
              ♣ K 9 6 4
  ♠ 10 8 5 4              ♠ J 6 2
  ♡ 10 4 2      N         ♡ Q 9
  ◇ 6        W     E      ◇ J 10 9 7 5 4 2
  ♣ Q 10 7 3 2   S        ♣ J
              ♠ K Q 9
              ♡ A K 8 7 5
              ◇ Q 8
              ♣ A 8 5
```

Both North-South pairs bid this hand unopposed, one to a sensible six hearts contract, the other to the very poor seven hearts. Both Wests led the ◇6.

At the table where the grand slam had been bid, declarer essentially had no option but to hope that the queen of hearts was doubleton. He won the opening lead, cashed the ace-king of trumps, and claimed thirteen tricks when the trumps behaved — seven hearts making.

At the second table, declarer won the diamond lead and laid down the ace of trumps. When East followed with the nine, declarer saw that he could take a safety play against a 4-1 trump break. He continued with a heart towards the jack. East won with the queen and returned a diamond, which West ruffed with the ten of hearts — six hearts down one!

South bid the hand better than his opponents and took an excellent safety play. His reward on this occasion? He lost 20 IMPs!

Key points

1. When you can afford a trump loser, give up that trick at a time when the defenders can do the least damage.

2. Finessing in the trump suit may be dangerous when a ruff is threatened. Consider playing the top honors instead.

3. Taking an anti-percentage trump finesse may be an effective safety play. It may keep the danger hand off lead, for example. It may also ensure the contract, whether or not the finesse succeeds.

A.

♠ A K Q 6 2
♡ J 4
◇ K J 7 2
♣ A 5

```
    N
 W     E
    S
```

◇ 10 led

♠ 9 3
♡ 8 6
◇ A Q 5
♣ K J 8 6 4 2

WEST	NORTH	EAST	SOUTH
	1♠	pass	2♣
pass	2◇	pass	3♣
pass	4♣	pass	5♣
all pass			

It should have been obvious to lead a heart on this bidding, but West places the ◇10 on the table. How will you play your 5♣ contract for maximum safety?

B.

      ♠ Q 8 2
      ♡ K 8 4
      ◇ 9 6 5 2
      ♣ K 7 5

	N	
W		E
	S	

♠J led

      ♠ 7 5
      ♡ A Q 6 5 2
      ◇ A K
      ♣ A Q 8 2

The defenders persist with spades against 4♡ and you ruff the third round. When you cash the king and ace of trumps, West shows out on the second round. How will you continue?

C.

      ♠ A 8 7
      ♡ Q 9 5 4 3
      ◇ Q J 3
      ♣ 8 5

	N	
W		E
	S	

♠5 led

      ♠ Q 3
      ♡ A 10 8 7 6
      ◇ A K 8 6 5
      ♣ 7

You reach a solid-looking four hearts and West leads the ♠5. How will you play the contract for maximum safety?

Answers

A. If the defenders had cashed two heart tricks, you would have taken the percentage play in the trump suit — ace, then low to the jack. After a diamond lead you can improve your prospects by combining two possibilities. You should cash the king and ace of trumps, winning immediately when the queen is doubleton in either hand. If trumps are 3-2 but the queen does not fall, you need to throw a heart on either spades or diamonds. Which should you choose? You should play on spades. You only need the defender with the last trump to follow to two rounds in that suit, before you throw a heart on the third round. If you played on diamonds, you would need the key defender to follow to three rounds.

B. You must make plans for the possible loser on the fourth round of clubs. If the suit breaks 3-3, all will be well. If East (the defender with the long trumps) holds four clubs, you will be able to ruff your last club. Even if East holds only two clubs, you can still make the contract. Suppose this is the full layout:

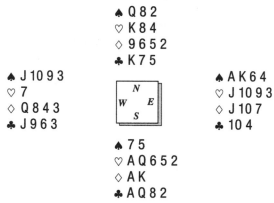

You ruff the third spade and play the king and ace of trumps, exposing the bad break. You then cash the ace and king of clubs and lead a third round of the suit through East, the defender with the long trumps. If East ruffs, this will be his last trick; you will win his return and draw the outstanding trump. If East discards on the third round of clubs, you will win with the ♣Q and ruff your last club. East is welcome to overruff, because you will be condensing two losers into one. Game made!

C. There is a possible safety play in the trump suit, to guarantee a maximum of one loser: you play low to the ten. If this loses, the defenders' trumps will break 2-1. Should East show out on the first round of trumps, you will rise with the ace and lead back towards the queen. Is there anything else to consider? Yes, suppose you play low from dummy on the first trick. East may win with the king and switch to a singleton diamond (or to a diamond from a four-card holding). The 'safety play' in trumps may then be a misnomer. It could result in a ruff when trumps were 2-1 all along. For maximum safety, you should rise with dummy's ace of spades and play a trump to the ten.

More Bridge Books From Master Point Press

Murder at the Bridge Table by Matthew Granovetter
320pp., PB   Can$19.95   US$14.95

I Shot my Bridge Partner by Matthew Granovetter
384pp., PB   Can$19.95   US$14.95

Classic Kantar — *a collection of bridge humor* by Eddie Kantar
192pp., PB   Can$19.95   US$14.95

Around the World in 80 Hands by Zia Mahmood with David Burn
256pp., PB   Can$22.95   US$16.95

World Class — *conversations with the bridge masters* by Marc Smith
288pp., PB (photographs) Can$24.95   US$17.95

Countdown to Winning Bridge by Tim Bourke and Marc Smith
192pp., PB   Can $19.95   US$14.95

Partnership Bidding *a workbook* by Mary Paul
96pp., PB   Can $9.95   US $7.95

There Must Be A Way... *52 challenging bridge hands*
by Andrew Diosy (foreword by Eddie Kantar)
96pp., PB $ 9.95 US & Can.

You Have to See This... *52 more challenging bridge problems*
by Andrew Diosy and Linda Lee
96pp., PB   Can $12.95   US $9.95

Bridge, Zia... and me by Michael Rosenberg
(foreword by Zia Mahmood)
192pp., PB   Can $19.95   US$15.95

Easier Done Than Said *Brilliancy at the Bridge Table*
by Prakash. K. Paranjape
128pp., PB   Can $15.95   US $12.95

The Bridge Player's Bedside Book edited by Tony Forrester
256pp., HC   Can $27.95   US $19.95

Focus On Declarer Play by Danny Roth
128pp., PB   Can $12.95   US $9.95

Focus On Defence by Danny Roth
128pp., PB   Can $12.95   US $9.95

Focus On Bidding by Danny Roth
160pp., PB   Can $14.95   US $11.95

Challenge Your Declarer Play by Danny Roth (*available April, 2000*)
128pp., PB   Can. $12.95   US $ 9.95

The Complete Book of BOLS Bridge Tips edited by Sally Brock
176pp., PB (photographs)   Can $24.95   US$17.95

Bridge the Silver Way by David Silver
192pp., PB   Can $19.95   US $14.95

Tales out of School *'Bridge 101' and other stories*
by David Silver (foreword by Dorothy Hayden Truscott)
128pp., PB   Can $ 12.95   US$9.95

A Study in Silver *A second collection of bridge stories*
by David Silver
128pp., PB   Can $ 12.95   US$ 9.95

Competitive Bidding in the 21st Century by Marshall Miles
(*available July, 2000*)   240pp., PB Can $ 22.95 US $16.95

For more information
visit our website

www.pathcom.com/~raylee/